The Unfavorable Police Encounter

The Do's & Don'ts when stopped by Law Enforcement Officers

Eugene Butler Jr.

Eugene Butler, Jr.

To: Mr A. Howard

Thank you for your support
Be Safe
Trooper
Butler

The Unfavorable Police Encounter

The Do's & Don'ts when stopped by Law Enforcement Officers

Eugene Butler, Jr.

© 2020

Published by Butler Publishers

Layout by www.diverseskillscenter.com

Printed in the United States of America

U.S. Copyright No.

ISBN: 978-0-578-77488-6

Table of Contents

This book is dedicated to,

My grandmother Dora Butler who raise me.

My parents Eugene & Mary Frances Butler.

To Senia Ford, Minnie Roberts and Severia Wilson

Franklin

Introduction

"I believe that the most important element of the United States Criminal Justice System is the presumption of innocence. The notion that a person is innocent and must be treated until proven guilty in a court of law. Yet, when a defendant is brought before a judge in prison clothes, handcuffs, and shackles, his presumption of innocence is flushed down the toilet. He becomes guilty until he proves that he is innocent."

My law enforcement career started shortly after high school when I served three years in the United States Army as a military policeman. My military service included an additional twenty-seven years in the army reserve. Later, I was called to serve in Operation Desert Shield, otherwise known as Desert Storm, and the war on terror.

I received an honorable discharge from the military and served approximately three years with the Monticello and

Tallahassee, Florida Police Departments. I then served an additional two years with the Leon County Sheriff Department as a Deputy Sheriff. Afterward, I worked as a correctional officer for two years and then as a Florida State Trooper for another two years.

My specific duties as a police officer ranged from simple traffic stops, traffic accidents, detection of speeding motorists using radar detection, and monitoring for drivers under the influence (D.W.I.), investigations, and patrolling the community, preventing criminal activity, and protecting citizens from personal and property crimes.

Police cars have very distinguished signs that read "To Protect and Serve." This is the essence of law enforcement. Police departments all over America must gain public trust and respect each other with the highest degree of integrity possible. As a former police officer, I wrote this book to enlighten others about unfavorable encounters with "the men and women in blue."

I hope this book will give you an inside look into law enforcement operations and how the United States Constitution governs it.

Chapter 1

The Vetting Process for Police Officers

There are many people who are interested in becoming a police officer, but you may ask yourself, what does becoming a police officer entail? While working as a police officer, that same question was asked.

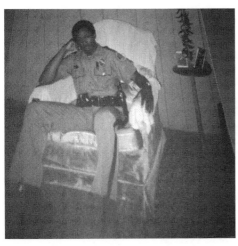

Some individuals say they went through the vetting process to become an officer, and they were rejected. The vetting process eliminates some candidates from law enforcement while allowing others into the profession, though some should not be allowed to become a police officer. The vetting process is not absolute in preventing police departments from hiring people in the wrong profession.

Now, new technology exposes the cruel treatment of individuals, especially that of black males. Because of technology, the police have used camera phones and brought to the forefront on a national and international level.

Many men and women are sincere and genuine about seeking a career in law enforcement. Let me share with you the reason I became interested in law enforcement.

I was around 12 years old. At that time, we had a TV that offered only three channels. While watching the CBS evening news, I saw a horrible scene: Vicious attack dogs were sicced on Black Americans for demonstrating in the State of Alabama. At that young age, I immediately knew that our country had a racial problem, especially in the southern states where I was born and raised.

By today's standards, what I witnessed then was an act of terror perpetrated by the police and fire department. The only solution I could think of was becoming a police officer to make a difference, knowing it would take decades to rectify these injustices, and cruel and inhumane treatment of black people in our communities, by our police departments throughout this country.

As I grew older, I learned that the police was operating on the authority of their department heads, chiefs, sheriffs, and local politicians rather than the Constitution, state laws, the department's standard of operations or SOPs, and the training received, all of which represent citizens fairly.

These department heads have their hidden agendas and their ideas of what is correct or incorrect. In other words, they are operating in the "gray area"!

In the fifth grade, I was selected by my teacher to be a school safety patrolman. My responsibility was to write down students' names that talked excessively when the teacher wasn't in the classroom. Riding home on the bus, I was also required to add students' names to my list if they moved from seat to seat, and the ones that were talking too loudly, which would then be turned into the principle.

During school hours, I would walk the halls looking for students that were late or skipping class. Sometimes, I monitored lunch lines for excessive playing and made sure the order was kept, earning me the title, School Safety Guard. In my sophomore year of high school, a deputy caught my eye as he was directing traffic. I remember so well because he was dressed professionally and was sharp as he moved the traffic swiftly and smoothly. At that moment, I realized that law enforcement was the career I wanted to pursue.

Approximately two weeks later, I got a chance to talk with the deputy, Deputy G. Proctor. I wanted to know how he became a deputy sheriff and how I could become a deputy. Seeing as in how I was only in high school, his response to me was, "Young man, stay out of trouble." My next question was, "Can I ride with you after school sometimes?"

At that time, it was called "The Ride Along." To ride with Deputy Proctor, I had to get permission from the Sheriff himself. Deputy Proctor had already predicted that he would give me his approval, which made me feel better about asking him.

He gave me the yes I needed to hear, and I felt like it was confirmation that I was not only making the right decision, but also that I would enjoy this line of work, and the Sheriff seemed glad that I had asked to be a ride-along. Fridays, Saturdays, and Sundays were the most enjoyable.

I played gospel music every Sunday from 6 am to 6 pm for WWSD, a local radio station in Monticello, Florida, during high school. Upon completion of high school, I worked full time at Winn-Dixie. A few months later, I decided to ask the Sheriff for a deputy position. He said to me, "Young man, I wouldn't be able to sleep at night knowing you are out there with a gun at your side." I thought to myself, Sheriff, can't you take a sleeping pill? I'll have a job, and you, sir, can get your rest. I was serious about my solution but lacked the nerve to express this to the Sheriff.

A few weeks passed by, and I posed the same question to the chief of police. By this time, all the deputies knew me. The chief replied, "I'll tell you what, Eugene. You go into the military for three years, and when you get out, come see me, and I'll hire you as an officer."

Three years later, upon my military completion with an honorable discharge, the chief would keep his word. Having him keep his word inspired me to do my best at my job.

In the military, after completing basic training, I was assigned to Fort Gordon, Georgia. After completing my advanced training, my duty station was Fort Ord, California. I felt at home in California; the weather was similar to

Florida. The one significant difference was the earthquakes, which played a large role in my decision to return to Florida.

While in the military, I was offered a chance to attend the LAPD academy. Being a military police officer was my first glance into police work. That experience enhanced my ability and my understanding of the role I would play in our society.

I worked with the civilian population from surrounding cities, such as Monterey, Carmel, and Seaside, alongside forty thousand troops. After a year and a half, I received orders for a twelve-month tour in Korea. Four months after leaving the Republic of Korea, I was stationed at Fort Bennie, Georgia, where I was discharged.

I couldn't wait to show my D.D. form 214 to the police chief in my hometown of Monticello. I sponsored myself and completed the police academy in Midway, Florida. Upon my completion, the chief was true to his word and hired me as an officer.

I would later apply to become an officer with the Florida Highway Patrol. Even though I was a certified police officer, I was treated as if I had no law enforcement training or experience in the academy. I was practically a new recruit. Though I knew I was more advanced than the recruits, I accepted the system and the training to become a state trooper.

The steps to the hiring process are as follows

1. Fill out the application

2. The written examination

3. Complete a physical examination

4. A physical agility tests

5. Background investigation

6. A 4-hour polygraph examination

7. An interview boards

The vetting process takes approximately six months to complete. During any step of the process, one can be disqualified at any time. Once you pass all the qualifications, you are invited by mail with the date and time to report to the Florida Highway Patrol Academy to begin your training. The letter consists of things to bring, what to expect, and explains starting a physical exercise program before reporting to the academy. Like our former President, Barack Obama said, I was "fired up and ready to go."

After completing the academy, I was given my first assignment at Troop-B with a reporting date. A Caucasian American trooper came to the academy for in-service training, and while there, he inquired about the African American trooper assigned to his troop. We met and had the chance to talk a few minutes during a break. He seemed to be a nice person, and I felt good about reporting to Troop B.

Word gets out about what type of officer you are and what you represent, and I was known for being fair but firm in enforcing the law. My forte was detecting drunk drivers and people who had warrants for their arrest. There was a feeling of enjoyment while walking the beat, stopping, and talking to people on and off duty. It helps develop a dialogue between the police force and the community from what I saw from the chief to the patrolman.

One of the key elements of policing is to have your hands on the pulse of your community you serve. To regain the people's trust, we, the police-community, needed to be addressed with more empathy and sincerity, especially in training.

Chapter 2

Police Situations

This chapter consists of four scenarios from a police officer's perspective: the unfavorable police encounter. Each of these situations is my real encounters as a police officer. After each crisis, ask yourself were the officer's actions:

1. Reasonable or unreasonable?

2. Constitutional or unconstitutional?

3. Justifiable for an arrest or not?

Situation #1

The time was 10 pm. While on patrol, I stopped a vehicle for excessive speed, 15 mph over the posted speed limit. The stop was made approximately 10 miles outside of the city limits in a very dark and remote area.

As I approached, I saw and felt that the car's trunk was closed and secure, the driver was the only person in the vehicle, and his window rolled down. I asked to see his driver's license, registration, and insurance card. As he was retrieving these items, I informed him of the reason I stopped him. (He was clocked on the radar going 70 mph in a 55-mph zone). I asked him, "Do you have a reason for traveling over the posted speed limit?" Handing me the information I had asked for, he replied, "I didn't know I was speeding."

At that time, I asked the driver to step out of the car. He cooperated and stepped out of the car. I observed him in full view and decided that he was not impaired; he appeared to be an average individual. As I was writing him a citation, he says to me, "If we were in Tampa, I'd kick your ass."

I immediately drew my service revolver from my holster and held it pointed to the ground. With a clear, audible voice, I told the driver, "We are not in Tampa. I'll kill you right where you're standing. Don't say another word."

I re-holstered my weapon and completed the speeding citation. I explained the citation and asked him to sign it, which he did.

In this situation, this individual not only put the trooper in great danger but also himself. The driver displayed a bad attitude that put himself in jeopardy of being seriously injured or causing the trooper harm. The driver's decision to threaten the trooper could have altered his or the trooper's life forever. This situation is a prime example of an unfavorable police encounter that was utterly avoidable.

What the driver should have done was to cooperate and follow the officer's instructions we gave without verbally threatening the officer with bodily harm. Behaviors like this are never acceptable.

If you disagreed with the way an officer handles a situation, things you can do to avoid confrontation are

1. Request to speak with the immediate supervisor

2. File a complaint with the Department (Internal Affairs)

3. Take your case to court and let the judge come to a legal resolution.

All of the above are acceptable ways to handle an in-agreeable situation with an officer. Never physically or verbally threaten an officer. The possibility of anything good coming from your actions is zero to none.

Situation #2

Being dispatched to the scene of an accident, upon arrival, I found the driver of an overturned pick-up truck lying on the ground along a fence line, receiving medical assistance from two emergency medical technicians. Approximately 15-20 bystanders were on the scene of the accident, none of which had witnessed the accident.

As I approached, I quickly noticed an African American male picking up tools off the ground along the scene. I immediately asked the person to put the items down and stand with the other bystanders away from the scene. At this time, a man in the crowd went into a rage, using profanity toward me and telling me what he would do to me using every unkind word he could think of. As I received information for the accident report, I continued to keep an eye on this loud and belligerent individual. I figured he was letting off some steam and would stop soon enough. After a couple of minutes of continued unruly behavior, I knew I had to deal with this individual. I approached him and said, "Sir, you are under arrest for interference with a law enforcement officer in the performance of his duties." He then stepped toward me in a threatening manner.

At that time, my options for defense weapons were minimal compared to current police gear. I drew my revolver and pulled the hammer back. This man's brother, seeing how out of control he was, grabbed him and placed him in the back of my patrol car. While en route to the jail, he apologized and expressed how he didn't want to go to jail. The subject was intoxicated and appeared to have had smoked an unknown substance.

The consequences of his actions could have ended with one of us getting seriously injured, or worse, killed. His actions led to an unnecessary arrest. In most cases, arrests can be avoided by staying calm and following instructions. This situation went from an accident scene to a crime scene. The belligerent bystander was charged with aggravated assault on a police officer. The driver was later charged with a DWI (driving while intoxicated).

Situation #3

The road was still wet from the heavy rain when I pulled over a vehicle for speeding. The car pulled over onto a muddy shoulder, and I immediately got out of my car to speak with the driver. The driver was a young, black male, well dressed, and well mannered. A speeding citation was issued, and after explaining the citation and having him sign, he returned to his car. He sped off, slinging mud all over the hood and windshield of my patrol car. The subject was stopped a second time and arrested for reckless driving, which required his vehicle to be towed. Once again, this situation could have been avoided if he had only driven away without making a splash.

Situation #4

While on patrol, I encountered a 19-year-old white male who weighed no more than 110 pounds. I had pulled him over because I had clocked him by radar driving 92 mph in a 55-

mph zone. When asked why he was driving so fast, he replied that he was on probation and needed to be in place by a specific time and that this was his second speeding citation that day. I decided to place him under arrest for reckless driving.

When I communicated this to him, he pulled me into a headlock. I pulled my service revolver with my left hand while defending myself with my right hand. I managed to put him into a hammerlock position and regain control of this unfavorable police encounter.

While struggling with the suspect, I observed an eighteen-wheeler on the opposite side of the highway coming to a stop. The traffic was light as the eighteen-wheeler driver made his way toward us with a lead pipe. I was afraid of the possibility that I not only had one person to deal with but another that was heading my way. I wasn't sure if the truck driver was a friend or a foe.

Losing hold on the suspect, he managed to escape from me on foot into the woods, across the highway. I quickly called for backup with a K-9 Unit. After a few minutes, the K-9 Unit arrived on the scene. The suspect surrendered, and I was able to take him into custody. Ultimately, this individual's car was towed, and he was charged with:

1. Reckless driving

2. Resisting arrest, and

3. Battery on a law enforcement officer

He committed a serious offense by putting his hands on a law enforcement officer in a threatening manner. The training I received in the academy did indeed support the use of deadly force during this encounter. I didn't feel the use of deadly force was necessary in this case, but if the subject had been larger or stronger, more than likely, it would have ended with lethal force.

The Police Officer Duty Gear

Outlined here is the duty gear every police officer is equipped with. His equipment is used to assist the police officer in his duties, from no force to deadly force.

1. Handgun and holster
2. Magazine
3. Ammunition
4. Taser and holster
5. Duty belt
6. Belt keepers
7. Flashlight and holder

8. OC Spray and pouch
9. Handcuffs and pouch
10. Baton and holder
11. Radio and pouch
12. Glove and pouch
13. Armor vest
14. Tactical boots

Anytime someone comes into contact with a police officer or commits a criminal act, they have just entered the triangle. The triangle below refers to our legal system.

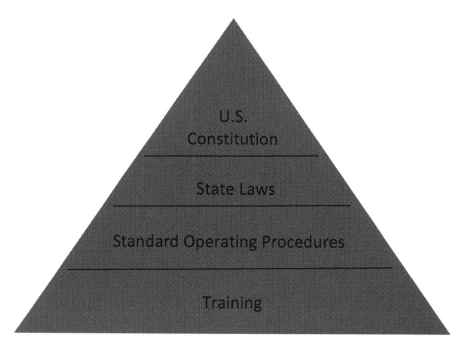

U.S. Constitution

State Laws

Standard Operating Procedures

Training

The outcome of your encounter will be determined by whether you remain in the triangle or you exit it. People who work inside this triangle are governed by it 24 hours 7 days a week, and they are held accountable for their actions and reactions. Police officers are required to complete training and follow the department's Standard of Operations (SOP).

As a citizen, it is your duty and your right to know your local police department's SOP. In its entirety, the U.S. Constitution is written in this book as a reminder to you of your constitutional rights. This triangle is the legal umbrella that law enforcement operates under.

Chapter 3

"You Are Under Arrest"

Phase I

The next thing you hear is your Miranda Rights being read to you, which were established in a 1966 U.S. Supreme Court ruling in the case of Miranda v. Arizona.

These rights State

➤ You have the right to…

   1. Remain silent

   2. Don't speak

   3. Be quiet

➤ Anything you say can and will be used against you in a court of law…

   1. Remain silent

   2. Don't speak

   3. Be Quiet

➤ You have the right to speak to a lawyer and to have a lawyer present when you are being questioned

   1. Remain silent

   2. Don't speak

   3. Be quiet

➤ If you want a lawyer before or during questioning but cannot afford to hire a lawyer, one will be appointed to represent you at no cost before any questioning.

    1. Remain silent

    2. Don't speak

    3. Be quiet

➤ If you answer questions without a lawyer present, you still have the right to stop answering questions at any time.

    1. Remain silent

    2. Don't speak

    3. Be quiet

Waiver of Rights

➤ Do you understand each of the rights I have explained to you?

    Adults may answer "yes" or "no."

➤ If yes, having these rights in mind, do you now wish to answer any questions?

    Just say, "no."

➤ If yes, do you now wish to answer questions without a lawyer present?

    "No," "No," "No."

➢ If a juvenile (ages 14-17), do you now wish to answer questions without your parents, guardians, or custodial parents?

"No," "No," "No."

Your rights fall under the Fifth Amendment of the United States Constitution: "No person shall be held to answer for a capital, or otherwise, infamous crime, nor shall any person be subject for the same offense to be twice put in jeopardy of life or limb; nor shall they be compelled in any criminal case to be a witness against himself, nor be deprived of life, liberty, or property without due process of law."

According to the Fifth Amendment, we are all guaranteed the due process of law, regardless of our financial (or any other) status. We know that these words are just not valid. In my opinion, the remedy to our disparate criminal justice system is for people to not commit unlawful acts, but this is an unrealistic solution.

Remember when you were given your Miranda rights, and you insisted on talking when you were told to remain silent? Do not say to the police your involvement in the crime before the officer questions you. Remember, anything you say can and will be used against you in a court of law. Whatever you say to the police will be repeated in court, along with the date, time, and location it was told. This is real evidence that is seldom used to exonerate you but is often used to convict you.

Phase II

Misdemeanor: A crime less serious than a felony that carries a possible jail sentence of one year or less.

Felony: a crime considered severe, carrying a punishment of a term in prison or capital punishment if that State has capital punishment.

A felony has been committed in the police officer's jurisdiction of the court, and the officer has probable cause that the suspect committed the crime. You (the suspect) are taken into custody by law enforcement, and you are informed of the charge or the crime for which you are being arrested. After being processed into the local jail, you can post a bond and be released or remain in jail until your first appearance in court, within 24 hours of your arrest. The judge will inform you, the defendant or accused, of the charges that have been placed against you. He also advises you of your rights and the opportunity to post bail.

At your first appearance, criminal charges could be dropped. You should have an attorney present with you at this stage to make sure your constitutional rights are protected. With proper representation, you could be released. The arresting officer is no longer directly involved in this part of the process. All reports are approved, and evidence is turned into the proper authorities, and the officer goes back on patrol.

Phase III
Trial or Plea Negotiation

If you choose to go to trial, you need to know Amendment VI in the U.S. Constitution that states all criminal prosecutions, "the accused shall enjoy the right to a speedy and public trial, by an impartial jury of the state and district wherein the crime shall have been committed, which district shall have been previously ascertained by law and to be informed of the nature and cause of the accusation; to be confronted with the witnesses against him; to have compulsory process for obtaining witnesses in his favor, and to have the assistance of legal counsel for his defense."

If you choose to go to trial, make sure all of your rights in Amendment VI are being adhered to. A nolo contendere plea allows a defendant to accept conviction on a charge while neither admitting nor denying commission of a crime. As a result of a trial, three key things from our criminal justice system can happen.

1. You can be found guilty
2. You can be found not guilty
3. A hung jury/retrial

Phase IV
Preparing for a Criminal Trial

Let's not kid ourselves; this is an awfully expensive process. Some people sell their homes, deplete their savings accounts, and borrow large sums of money to defend themselves or their loved ones in a trial, but it's in your best interest to have an attorney of your choice before your trial begins.

These are a few things you will face during a criminal trial. The rule of evidence: the court will determine the admissibility of evidence at the hearing. The evidence or the lack thereof will determine if a trial will take place or not. Under your constitutional rights, you have an allotted amount of time before trial. Make sure you are aware of the time your case must go to trial. This falls under the 6th Amendment or the Speedy Trial Act of 1974. This same amendment outlines the guidelines of jury selection; this ensures selecting an impartial jury of peers.

This process is known as the voire dire examination. The prosecutor and defense attorney can dismiss a juror for peremptory challenge or challenge for cause. A juror is believed to be biased, which then prevents them from being impartial. The jury and alternates are selected, and they are sworn in by the court. The jury can then be sequestered or isolated from the public during the trial.

The prosecution and the defense will describe the facts that each side will present to prove or disprove the case. Under the Good Faith ethical requirement, each side can only introduce evidence to present during the trial. The prosecutor and defense attorney present their evidence to the jury. I refer to this as the Heartbeat of the Trial; your freedom hangs on how well your attorney can prove your innocence. The closing arguments occur when the trial has concluded. Here, the prosecutor and the defense give the jury a summation of the case. This is the last opportunity for attorneys to persuade the jury to convict or not to convict the defendant.

Phase V

During this phase, the judge will provide detailed instructions to the jury on legal issues concerning the case. He then will instruct them to deliberate until a verdict is unanimously rendered.

During jury deliberation, all evidence presented during the trial will be considered. This will help the jury reach a verdict. The verdict will either result in an acquittal — the defendant is "not guilty" for a conviction.

A hung jury happens when a jury cannot reach a unanimous verdict. A retrial is then warranted. A mistrial occurs as a result of some circumstance that makes it impossible to continue a fair trial. Not guilty because of insanity is a ruling that occurs when the defendant does not have the mental capacity to be held criminally responsible for their actions. In this case, the defendant is guilty but mentally ill. The defendant will still face punishment, but there is more emphasis on treating them.

The judge receives a pre-sentence report to aid in the appropriate sentencing, and the victim/s are given a chance to express the impacts of the defendant's actions and its effect on their lives.

Chapter 4

Your Attitude

Let's take a close look at the word attitude and how it is related to you if you find yourself in an unfavorable police encounter.

Attitude is defined as how one is placed, how a person holds or carries themselves, and a frame of mind affecting one's thoughts or behaviors.

For a moment, let's concentrate on your attitude when you are being approached by a police officer or while driving when the blue lights are turned on behind you. Having a good attitude and mannerisms go a long way in showing our first-responders the respect they are due, and in turn, for them to show the respect due to the people they serve. This is an example of how an encounter with the police should go when stopped for a traffic violation.

Usually, when you are stopped, you hear these things,

1. Good evening sir or ma'am

2. May I see your driver's license, vehicle registration, and your insurance card, please.

3. I stopped you because I clocked you on the radar doing 40 mph in a 25-mph zone. Do you have a reason for exceeding the posted speed limit?

This allows the individual to express their reasons for traveling in access to the speed limit.

Most people I spoke to don't get their vehicles calibrated every 6 months as they should. For example, if the tires have been changed, that would alter the calibration of that vehicle. Since the tires have been changed from the original factory size, the speed odometer will show your speed at 25 mph, while at the same time, the police radar will clock you at 35 mph.

When a police officer approaches someone with a bad attitude or behavior, it only elevates the officer's need to go into self-protection mode. Your bad attitude puts your life, as well as the police officers, at risk. Remember, police officers, do not have a crystal ball that tells them that you are just having a bad day. Your demeanor and attitude say a lot about you before you say anything.

More often than not, an officer decides on how to handle the situation based on your attitude and demeanor. You must make sure the officer's instructions are clear, and you understand what is being asked of you, so you can be in complete compliance with his instructions. Failure to follow instructions can result in someone's death, injury, or arrest. For the safety of both the police officer and you, the citizen, everyone is calm and polite during an encounter with the police.

Most of the situations we have read about and seen on the news turn ugly because of miscommunication or just failure to comply with police instructions. Some of these situations are blatantly caused by the misconduct of the police officer. Wait patiently for instructions from the officer to ensure you understand and comply with proper procedures. The point is to remain calm, cool, and professional.

Police officers are in charge of the scene in most encounters. Give officers the respect and courtesy that are due them. If you feel that you were disrespected by the police officer, do not get into a verbal altercation with the police. Take your complaint to the officer's supervisor or to the internal affairs office. The police department has policies and procedures to help resolve differences between the police department and the community they serve.

Most people drive every day without being stopped by a police officer but keep in mind when you are operating a motor vehicle, you are subject to being stopped by the police for traffic violations or other miscellaneous offenses. When you are pulled over and your attitude is not at your best, take a moment and make an attitude adjustment. Tell yourself I am not in charge of this situation.

Have your driver's license, vehicle registration, and insurance card ready to present to the officer on demand. There should be an easily accessible and visible area in the vehicle to place these documents to be there and ready to be presented when asked. U.S. citizens with no criminal history or intent should not be injured or killed because of false movement or a misunderstanding.

Whether you can justify the movement or your actions, it is up to the officer to establish your intent, leading to unforeseen circumstances, to kill a person over a non-threatening situation. No one should get hurt if no one's life is in danger. Deadly force should be a last resort.

Here are the options for you to consider. If you feel like you were treated unfairly by a police officer, take your complaints to the department's internal affairs. Even if you are arrested, an officer has no excuse to display a bad attitude toward you. When you encounter a police officer with a bad attitude, remain silent, do nothing to further antagonize the police officer, and cause the situation to get out of control.

Citizens and police are held accountable for their actions. Too often, the police's misconduct is overlooked or swept under the rug, meaning nothing is being said or done about it. The police department wants citizens to be vigilant; see something say something. When you see or are a victim of an officer's conduct unbecoming, report it to the appropriate authorities.

It only takes a few police officers with a bad attitude to give a bad impression of the whole police department. It's not fair to the officers that are professionally doing their job. It is time to stop officers with bad attitudes from hiding behind good and caring officers.

Chapter 5

Weapons and Firearms: Justifiable Use of Force

Florida Statute 776.012. Use of force in defense of a person.

A person is justified in the use of force, except deadly force against another, where and to the extent that the person reasonably believes that such conduct is necessary to defend himself or another against such others imminent use of unlawful force. However, he is justified in using deadly force only if he reasonably believes that such force is necessary to prevent imminent death or great bodily harm to himself or another or prevent the imminent commission of a forcible felony.

F.S. 776.05 Law Enforcement Officers' Use Of Force in Making an Arrest

A law enforcement officer, or any person he has summoned or directed to assist him, needs not retreat, or desist from efforts to make a lawful arrest because of resistance or threatened resistance to the arrest. He is justified in the use of any force:

1. He reasonably believes to be necessary to defend himself or another from bodily harm while making the arrest.

2. When necessarily committed to retaking felons who have escaped, or

3. When necessarily committed to arresting felons fleeing from justice. However, this sub-sectional shall not constitute a defense in any civil action for damages brought for the wrongful use of deadly force unless the use of deadly force was necessary to prevent the arrest from being defeated by such flight and when feasible, some warning had been given, and;

a. The officer reasonably believes that the fleeing felon poses a threat of death or serious physical harm to the officer or others, or

b. The officer reasonably believes that the fleeing felon has committed a crime involving the infliction or threatened infliction of serious physical harm to another person.

F.S. 790.02 Officer to Arrest Without Warrant and Upon Probable Cause

The carrying of a concealed weapon is declared a breach of peace. Any officer authorized to make arrests under the laws of this State may make arrests without warrant of persons violating the provision of Florida status, when a said officer has reasonable grounds or probable cause to believe that the offense of carrying a concealed weapon is being committed.

F.S. 790.06 License to Carry Concealed Weapon or Firearm

The Department of State is authorized to issue licenses to carry concealed weapons or concealed firearms to persons qualified. Each such license must bear a color photograph of the licensee. A concealed weapons or concealed firearms are a handgun, electronic weapon or device, tear gas gun, knife, or billie, but the term does not include a machine gun.

F.S. 790.07 Furnishing Weapons to Minors Under 18 Years of Age

Whoever sells, hires, barters, lends, or gives any minor under 18 years of age any pistol, dirk, electric weapon or device, or other arm or weapon, other than an ordinary pocket knife, without permission of the parent of such minor, or the person having charge of such minor, or sells, hires, barters, lends, or gives to any person of unsound mind an electric weapon or device or any dangerous weapon, other than an ordinary pocket knife, is guilty of a misdemeanor of the first degree.

F.S. 790.174 Safe Storage of Firearms Required

A person who stores or leaves, on a premise under his control, a loaded firearm, and who knows or reasonably should know that a minor is likely to gain access to the firearm without the lawful permission of the minor's parent or the person having charge of the minor, or without the supervision required by law, shall keep the firearm in a securely locked box or container or in a location which a reasonable person would believe to be secure or shall secure it with a trigger lock. Violation of this law is a misdemeanor of the second degree.

F.S. 790.23 Felons; Possession of Firearms or Electric Weapons or Devices Unlawful

It is unlawful for any person who has been convicted of a felony in the courts of this State or of a crime against the United States, which is designated as a felony, or convicted of an offense in any other state, territory, or country punishable by imprisonment for a term exceeding 1 year to own or to have in his care, custody, possession, or control, a firearm or electric weapon or device, or to carry a concealed weapon, including all tear gas guns and chemical weapons or devices. This section shall not apply to a person convicted of a felony whose civil rights have been restored. Any person convicted of violating this section is guilty of a felony of the second degree.

F.S. 790.24 Report of Medical Treatment of Gunshot Wounds; Penalty for Failure to Report

Any physician, nurse, or employee thereof, and any employee of a hospital, sanitarium, clinic, or nursing home knowingly treating any person suffering from a gunshot wound or other wound indicating violence, or receiving a request for such treatment, shall report the same immediately to the Sheriff's department of the country in which said treatment is administered or request therefore received. Therefore, any such person willfully failing to report such treatment or request is guilty of a misdemeanor of the first degree.

Though these statutes are exclusive to Florida, the average citizen should be familiar with their own states' statutes and laws on weapons and firearms. This book is designed to be a guide to help you familiarize yourself with the workings of the police. Remember, each State is different.

The F.B.I.'s Policy on the Use of Deadly Force

The F.B.I.'s policy is that agents are not to shoot any person except as necessary in self-defense, where they reasonably believe they or another are in danger of death or grievous bodily harm. The term "self-defense" also includes the right to defend another person against what is reasonably perceived as an immediate danger of death or grievous bodily harm to that person from (their) assailant.

Emphasis must be placed on planning arrests so that the maximum pressure placed on the individual being sought will afford him no opportunity to either resist or flee. Any situation of this type can deteriorate instantly, and continuing alertness, extreme care, and good judgment will better prepare our agents to control the situation.

Where the lawless person initiates action to cause physical harm, there should be no hesitancy in using such force as is necessary to bring such a person effectively and expeditiously under control. Good training can bring such a person under control. Good training and experience in arrest situations must be relied on to provide a proper response when confronted with deadly force situations. Many situations in which agents may draw their weapons were making an apprehension and without being confronted with existing deadly force. This is a judgment question, which must be evaluated in terms of the individual or individuals to be apprehended. The circumstances under which the apprehension is being made; no warning shots are to be fired by agents to stop a fleeing person or any other purpose.

If police departments used these policies alone, many lives would be saved, especially black lives.

Chapter 6

Outline of Facts

NAACP/Criminal Justice Fact Sheet

Incarceration Trends in America

➤ From 1980 to 2008, the number of people incarcerated in America quadrupled from roughly 500,000 to 2.3 million people.

➤ Today, the U.S. is 5% of the world's population and has 25% of its prisoners.

➤ Combining the number of people in prison and in jail with those under parole or probation supervision, 1 in every 31 adults or 3.2% of the population is under some form of correctional control.

Racial Disparities in Incarceration

➤ African Americans now constitute nearly 1 million of the total 2.3 million incarcerated population

➤ African Americans are incarcerated at nearly six times the rate of whites.

➢ Together, African Americans and Hispanics comprised 58% of all prisoners in 2008, even though African Americans and Hispanics make up approximately a quarter of the U.S. population.

➢ According to Unlocking America, if African Americans and Hispanics were incarcerated at the same rates as whites, today's prison and jail populations would decline by approximately 50%.

➢ 1 in 6 black men had been incarcerated as of 2001. If current trends continue, 1 in 3 black males born today can expect to spend time in prison during his lifetime.

➢ 1 in 100 African American women is in prison.

➢ Nationwide, African Americans represent 26% of juvenile arrests, 44% of youth detained, 46% of the youth who are judicially waived to criminal court, and 58% of the youth admitted to state prisons.

Drug Sentencing Disparities

➢ About 14 million whites and 2.6 million African Americans report using an illicit drug

➤ 5 times as many whites are using drugs as African Americans, yet African Americans are sent to prison for drug crimes at 10 times the whites' rate.

➤ African Americans represent 12% of the total population of drug users, but 38% of those are arrested for drug offenses, and 59% of those are in state prison for drug offenses.

➤ African Americans serve virtually as much time in prison for a drug offense (58.7 months) as whites do for violent offenses (61.7 months).

➤ In 2002, blacks constituted more than 80% of the people sentenced under the federal crack cocaine laws. They served substantially more time in prison for drug offenses than whites, even though more than two-thirds of crack cocaine users in the U.S. are white or Hispanic.

Contributing Factors

➤ Inner-city crimes are prompted by social and economic isolation

➤ The "Get Tough On Crime" and "War On Drugs" policies

- ➢ Mandatory minimum sentencing, especially disparities in sentencing for crack and powder cocaine possession.
- ➢ The "Three Strikes" habitual offender policies
- ➢ Zero Tolerance policies as a result of perceived problems of school violence/adverse effects on black children

Effects of Incarceration

- ➢ Jail reduces the work time of young people over the next decade by 25-30% compared with arrested youths who were not incarcerated.
- ➢ Jails and prisons are recognized as settings where society's infectious diseases are highly concentrated.
- ➢ Prison has not been proven as rehabilitation for behavior, as two-thirds of prisoners will offend again.

The Cost of Incarceration

- ➢ About $70 billion are spent on corrections yearly
- ➢ Prisons and jails consume a growing portion of the nearly $200 billion we spend annually on public safety [1]

---

[1] "Criminal Justice Fact Sheet." NAACP. Accessed November 27, 2019. https://www.naacp.org/criminal-justice-fact-sheet/.

The Statistics

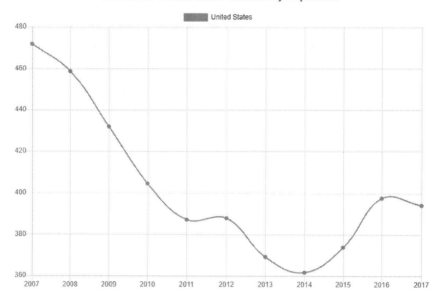

Rate of All Violent Crime Offenses by Population

According to the FBI's Uniform Crime Reporting (UCR),

there were more than 1.2 million violent crimes in 2017. Of these

1.2 million crimes, the largest percentage of violent crime

offenders and the largest percentage of violent crime victims in the

United States were white.

Let's look at the numbers:

- ➤ 176,967 whites were violent crime offenders, 233,708 whites were violent crime victims.

- ➤ 168,038 blacks were violent crime offenders, and 129,785 blacks were violent crime victims.

- ➤ Nationwide, law enforcement made an estimated 10,554,985 arrests in 2017. Of these arrests, 518,617 were for violent crimes, and 1,249,757 were for property crimes.

- ➤ The highest number of arrests were for drug abuse violations (estimated at 1,632,921 arrests), driving under the influence (estimated at 990,678), and larceny-theft (estimated at 950,357).

- ➤ The estimated arrest rate for the United States in 2017 was 3,251.5 arrests per 100,000 inhabitants. The arrest rate for violent crime (including murder and non-negligent manslaughter, rape, robbery, and aggravated assault) was 160.7 per 100,000 inhabitants. The arrest rate for property crime (burglary, larceny-theft, motor vehicle theft, and arson) was 388.7 per 100,000 inhabitants.

➢ Two-year arrest trends show that violent crime arrests increased by 0.8 percent in 2017 compared with 2016 arrests, and property crime arrests decreased by 6.7 percent compared with 2016 arrests.

➢ Arrests of juveniles for all offenses decreased 4.5 percent in 2017 compared with the 2016 number; adults' arrests decreased by 0.5 percent.

➢ Seventy-three percent of the persons arrested in the nation during 2017 were males. They accounted for 79.5 percent of persons arrested for violent crime, and 64.2 percent of persons arrested for property crime.

➢ In 2017, 68.9 percent of all persons arrested were White, 27.2 percent were Black or African American, and the remaining 3.9 percent were of other races. [2]

Now ask yourself, **what are the chances of these crimes happening to me?**

---

[2] "2018 Crime Statistics Released." FBI. FBI, September 30, 2019. https://www.fbi.gov/news/stories/2018-crime-statistics-released-093019.

What are the proper precautions to take to prevent these crimes from happening to you?

Every resident should have a directory of services and the number to each of their local departments.

Local Sheriff's Office

\# _____

Police Department

1. Victim Advocacy Unit

2. Sex crimes/Juvenile Unit

3. Homicide/Assault Unit

4. Property Crimes

5. Financial Crimes

6. Community Relations Unit

State Attorney General

Crime Victim Compensation

The Abuse Registry

Department of Corrections

Victim's Services

Center for Independent Living

MADD

Urban League

Big Bend

Refuge House/Rape Crisis

State Attorney's Office

Your universities or community college advocacy program

Check with your local law enforcement agency for a free security survey of your home.

Always be vigilant of your surroundings.

Do nothing to make it easier for an individual to make you a statistic: lock your doors and keep valuables out of sight, home, and in your car.

Take advantage of all electronic monitoring devices.

Glossary

Legal Terms You Should Know

Accessory — a person that helps someone else commit a crime, either before or after the crime.

Accomplice — a partner in a crime, a person who knowingly and voluntarily participates with another in a criminal activity.

Acquittal — A jury verdict that a criminal defendant is not guilty, or the finding of a judge that the evidence is insufficient to support a conviction.

Adult — a person 18 years of age or older

Aggravated Assault — an unlawful full attack by one person upon another for the purpose of inflicting severe or aggravated bodily injury.

Aid and Abet — to assist another person actively, knowingly, or intentionally in the commission or attempted commission of a crime

Alibi — a defense claim that the accused was somewhere else at the time a crime was committed.

Admissible — evidence that may be considered by a jury or judge in civil and criminal cases

Affidavit — a written or printed statement made under oath

Arraignment — a proceeding in which a criminal defendant is brought into court told of the charges in an indictment or information and asked to plead guilty, not guilty, or no contest.

Arrest — taking an adult or juvenile into physical custody by a police officer for the purpose of charging the person with a criminal offense

Assets — property of all kinds, including real and personal, tangible, and intangible

Assume — an agreement to continue performing duties under a contract or lease

Bench Trial — a trial without a jury, in which the judge serves as the fact-finder

Bench Warrant — an order issued by a judge for the arrest of a person

Booking — following an arrest, the process of photographing, fingerprinting, and identifying data of a suspect

Capital Offense — a crime punishable by death

Compensatory damages — monetary payment awarded for actual losses to persons or organizations, including intangible losses such as pain and suffering or absence of service

Concurrent Sentence — prison terms for two or more offenses to be served at the same time, rather than one after the other

Consecutive Sentence — prison terms for two or more offenses to be served one after the other

Conviction — a judgment of guilt against a criminal defendant

Corpus Delicti — the facts that show that a crime has occurred; "the body of the crime."

Crime — something you do, or don't do that breaks a law that says you can't do it or must do it

Cyber Crime — any crime perpetrated through the use of computer technology or the internet

Deadly force — that level of force likely to cause death or great

bodily harm, never justified in making an arrest for a misdemeanor

offense. Even in felony situations, officers may be held civilly or

criminally liable for negligence

Defendant — an individual or business against whom a lawsuit is

filed

Deposition — An oral statement made before an officer, authorized

by law, to administer oaths

Disorderly Conduct — any behavior that tends to disturb the

public peace or decorum, scandalize the community, or shock the

public sense of morality

Double jeopardy — putting a person on trial more than once for

the same crime

DNA (deoxyribonucleic acid) — enabling investigators to identify

suspects by comparing their unique individual genetic codes with

the codes found in hair, blood, skin, and semen

Due Process of Law — the right of all persons to receive the

guarantees and safeguards of the law and the judicial process, such as adequate notice, the assistance of counsel, and the right to remain silent, to a speedy and public trial, to an impartial jury, and to confront and secure witnesses

Entrapment— inducing a person to commit a crime so that criminal charges will be brought against them

Evidence— Information presented in testimony or in documents that are used to persuade the fact-finder (judge or jury) to decide the case of one side or other

Excessive force— the amount of force greater than that required to compel compliance from a willing or unwilling subject

Exclusionary rule— evidence obtained in violation of a criminal defendant's constitutional or statutory rights is not admissible at trial

Exhibits— physical evidence introduced at a hearing or trial

Felony— a serious crime, usually punishable by at least one year in prison

First Appearance— occurs within 24 hours of an arrest. Each suspect kept in jail must appear before a judge who establishes whether charges are reasonable. The judge will also consider whether a bond should be set, conditions of release, and appoint a defense attorney if the suspect can't afford one.

Fugitive — a person who flees from the one State to another to avoid prosecution

Grand Jury — a group of citizens who decide whether the prosecutor has enough evidence to pursue felony charges against a person

Hearsay — a witness who did not see or hear the incident in question but heard about it from someone else. With some exceptions, hearsay generally is not admissible as evidence at trial

Inculpatory Evidence — evidence indicating that a defendant did commit the crime

Indictment — a document that contains the felony charges that were voted by the grand jury

Jury — a group of persons selected to hear the evidence in a trial and render a verdict on matters of fact

Juvenile — a child under the age of 18 years

Misdemeanor— an offense punishable by one year of imprisonment or less

Motion— a request by a litigant to a judge for a decision on an issue relating to the case

Non-jury Trial— a case tried by a judge

Pain and suffering— physical or mental distress or torment caused by someone else's wrongful act

Plaintiff— a person or business that files a formal complaint with the court

Reasonable force— the police must only use a degree of force that is appropriate in a given situation and is not excessive

Sentence— the punishment ordered by a court for a defendant convicted of a crime

Subpoena— a command issued under a court's authority to a witness to appear and give testimony

Testimony— evidence presented orally by witnesses during trials or before grand juries

Verdict — the decision of a trial jury or a judge that determines the guilt or innocence of a criminal defendant

Victim — a person against whom a crime was committed. Some victims suffer physical injury or property damage, and some have a psychological injury or both

Voir dire — jury selection process of questioning perspective jurors, to ascertain their qualifications and determine any basis for the challenge

Warrant — court authorization, most often for law enforcement, to conduct a search or make an arrest

Witness — a person called upon by either side in a lawsuit to give testimony before the court or jury

Writ — a written order from a court demanding specific action by a person or an entity

Wrongful death — the death of another person as the result of a wrongful act

The Rights of the Victim of the Crime

Let me remind you of some of your rights as the victim:

In certain cases and at the earliest possible opportunity, the right To know if the person charged with an offense has tested positive for hepatitis and Human Immuno-deficiency Virus (HIV) infection.

The right To request in certain circumstances that the offender must attend a different school than the victim or siblings of the victim.

The right Of each victim or witness who has been scheduled to attend a criminal or juvenile justice proceeding to be notified as soon as possible by the agency.

The right To receive advance notification of judicial and post judicial proceedings that relate to the accused's arrest. Also, the release of the accused pending judicial proceedings and any modification of release conditions.

The right To not be excluded from any portion of any hearing trial or proceeding, pertaining to the offense, unless the court determines otherwise.

The right To a prompt return of property unless there is compelling law enforcement need to retain it.

The right To request a law enforcement agency to help you explain to employers and creditors that you may face additional burdens by taking time off from work to assist law enforcement. Law enforcement agencies shall inform you of your right to request and receive restitution and your rights of enforcement in the event, an offender does not pay. [3]

The right To receive information on available crisis intervention services and local community services. Information regarding the role of the victim in the criminal process. Along with the information regarding the stage of the criminal process.

The right To be informed, present, and heard, when relevant, during criminal processing, as long as the right does not interfere with the accused's constitutional rights.

The right To be notified when the offender escapes from custody

---

[3] "Crime Victims' Rights Act." The United States Department of Justice, July 22, 2016. https://www.justice.gov/usao/resources/crime-victims-rights-ombudsman/victims-rights-act.

The right Not to submit to a polygraph examination if you are the victim of a sexual offense.

All Amendments to the United States Constitution

Congress of the United States
begun and held at the City of New-York, on
Wednesday the fourth of March, one thousand seven
hundred and eighty-nine.

THE Conventions of a number of the States, having at the time of their adopting the Constitution, expressed a desire, in order to prevent misconstruction or abuse of its powers, that further declaratory and restrictive clauses should be added: And as extending the ground of public confidence in the Government, will best ensure the beneficent ends of its institution.

RESOLVED by the Senate and House of Representatives of the United States of America, in Congress assembled, two-thirds of both Houses concurring, that the following Articles be proposed to the Legislatures of the several States, as amendments to the Constitution of the United States, all, or any of which Articles, when ratified by three-fourths of the said Legislatures, to be valid to all intents and purposes, as part of the said Constitution; viz.

ARTICLES , in addition to an Amendment of the Constitution of the United States of America, proposed by Congress and ratified by the Legislatures of the several States, pursuant to the fifth Article of the original Constitution.

*Note: The following text is a transcription of
the first ten amendments to the Constitution in
their original form. These amendments have
ratified the fifteenth of December 1791, and
form what is known as the "Bill of Rights."*

AMENDMENT I

Congress shall make no law respecting an establishment of
religion, or prohibiting the free exercise thereof; or
abridging the freedom of speech, or of the press, or the
right of the people peaceably to assemble and to petition
the Government for a redress of grievances.

AMENDMENT II

A well-regulated Militia, being necessary to the security of
a free State, the people's right to keep and bear Arms, shall
not be infringed.

AMENDMENT III

No Soldier shall, in time of peace, be quartered in any
house, without the consent of the Owner, nor in time of
war, but in a manner to be prescribed by law.

AMENDMENT IV

The people's right to be secure in their persons, houses,
papers, and effects, against unreasonable searches and
seizures, shall not be violated. No Warrants shall issue, but
upon probable cause, supported by oath or affirmation,
particularly describing the place to be searched, and the
persons or things to be seized.

AMENDMENT V

No person shall be held to answer for a capital, or otherwise, infamous crime, unless on a presentment or indictment of a Grand Jury, except in cases arising in the land or naval forces, or in the Militia, when in actual service in time of war or public danger; nor shall any person be subject for the same offense to be twice put in jeopardy of life or limb; nor shall be compelled in any criminal case to be a witness against himself, nor be deprived of life, liberty, or property, without due process of law; nor shall private property be taken for public use, without just compensation.

AMENDMENT VI

In all criminal prosecutions, the accused shall enjoy the right to a speedy and public trial, by an impartial jury of the State and District wherein the crime shall have been committed, which District shall have been previously ascertained by law, and to be informed of the nature and cause of the accusation; to be confronted with the witnesses against him; to have compulsory process for obtaining witnesses in his favor, and to have the Assistance of Counsel for his defense.

AMENDMENT VII

In Suits at common law, where the value in controversy shall exceed twenty dollars, the right of trial by jury shall be preserved, and no fact tried by a jury, shall be otherwise re-examined in any Court of the United States, then according to the rules of the common law.

AMENDMENT VIII

Excessive bail shall not be required, nor excessive fines imposed, nor cruel and unusual punishments inflicted.

AMENDMENT IX

The enumeration in the Constitution of certain rights shall not be construed to deny or disparage others retained by the people.

AMENDMENT X

The powers not delegated to the United States by the Constitution, nor prohibited by it to the States, are reserved to the States respectively, or to the people.

AMENDMENT XI - Passed by Congress the fourth of March 1794. Ratified the seventh of February 1795.

Note: Article III, section 2, of the Constitution was modified by amendment 11.

The Judicial power of the United States shall not be construed to extend to any suit in law or equity, commenced or prosecuted against one of the United States by Citizens of another State, or by Citizens or Subjects of any Foreign State.

AMENDMENT XII - Passed by Congress the ninth of December 1803. Ratified on the fifteenth of June 1804.

Note: A portion of Article II, section 1 of the Constitution was superseded by the 12th amendment.

The Electors shall meet in their respective states and vote by ballot for President and Vice-President, one of whom, at least, shall not be an inhabitant of the same State with themselves; they shall name in their ballots the person voted for as President, and in distinct ballots the person voted for as Vice-President, and they shall make distinct lists of all persons voted for as President, and of all persons voted for as Vice-President, and of the number of votes for each, which lists they shall sign and certify, and transmit sealed to the seat of the Government of the United States, directed to the President of the Senate; -- the President of the Senate shall, in the presence of the Senate and House of Representatives, open all the certificates and the votes shall then be counted; -- The person having the greatest number of votes for President, shall be the President, if such number be a majority of the whole number of Electors appointed; and if no person have such majority, then from the persons having the highest numbers not exceeding three on the list of those voted for as President, the House of Representatives shall choose immediately, by ballot, the President. But in choosing the President, the votes shall be taken by states, the representation from each State having one vote; a quorum for this purpose shall consist of a member or members from two-thirds of the states, and a majority of all the states shall be necessary to a choice. [And if the House of Representatives shall not choose a President whenever the right of choice shall devolve upon them, before the fourth day of March next following, then the Vice-President shall act as President, as in case of the death or other constitutional disability of the President]. *The person having the greatest number of votes as Vice-President, shall be the Vice-President if such number be a majority of the whole number of Electors appointed, and if no person have a majority, then from the two highest numbers on the list, the Senate shall choose the Vice-President; a quorum for the purpose shall consist of two-thirds of the whole number of Senators, and a majority of the whole number shall be necessary to a choice. But no person constitutionally ineligible to the office of President shall be eligible to that of Vice-President of the United States.

Superseded by section 3 of the 20th amendment.

AMENDMENT XIII - Passed by Congress the thirty-first of January 1865. Ratified the sixth of December 1865.

Note: A portion of Article IV, section 2, of the Constitution was superseded by the 13th amendment.

Section 1.
Neither slavery nor involuntary servitude, except as a punishment for crime whereof the party shall have been duly convicted, shall exist within the United States or any place subject to their jurisdiction.

Section 2.
Congress shall have the power to enforce this article by appropriate legislation.

AMENDMENT XIV - Passed by Congress on the thirteenth of June 1866. Ratified the ninth of July 1868.

Note: Article I, section 2, of the Constitution was modified by section 2 of the 14th amendment.

Section 1.
All persons born or naturalized in the United States, and subject to the jurisdiction thereof, are citizens of the United States and of the State wherein they reside. No State shall make or enforce any law which shall abridge the privileges or immunities of citizens of the United States; nor shall any State deprive any person of life, liberty, or property, without due process of law; nor deny to any person within its jurisdiction the equal protection of the laws.

Section 2.
Representatives shall be apportioned among the several States according to their respective numbers, counting the whole number of persons in each State, excluding Indians not taxed. But when the right to vote at any election for the choice of electors for President and Vice-President of the United States, Representatives in Congress, the Executive and Judicial officers of a State, or the members of the Legislature thereof, is denied to any of the male inhabitants of such State, being twenty-one years of age,* and citizens of the United States, or in any way abridged, except for participation in rebellion, or other crime, the basis of representation therein shall be reduced in the proportion which the number of such male citizens shall bear to the whole number of male citizens twenty-one years of age in such State.

Section 3.
No person shall be a Senator or Representative in Congress, or elector of President and Vice-President, or hold any

office, civil or military, under the United States, or under any State, who, having previously taken an oath, as a member of Congress, or as an officer of the United States, or as a member of any State legislature, or as an executive or judicial officer of any State, to support the Constitution of the United States, shall have engaged in insurrection or rebellion against the same, or given aid or comfort to the enemies thereof. But Congress may, by a vote of two-thirds of each House, remove such disability.

Section 4.
The validity of the United States' public debt, authorized by law, including debts incurred for payment of pensions and bounties for services in suppressing insurrection or rebellion, shall not be questioned. But neither the United States nor any State shall assume or pay any debt or obligation incurred in aid of insurrection or rebellion against the United States, or any claim for the loss or emancipation of any slave. Still, all such debts, obligations, and claims shall be held illegal and void.

Section 5.
The Congress shall have the power to enforce, by appropriate legislation, the provisions of this article.

Changed by section 1 of the 26th amendment.

AMENDMENT XV - Passed by Congress the twenty-sixth of February 1869. Ratified the third of February 1870.

Section 1.
The right of citizens of the United States to vote shall not be denied or abridged by the United States or by any State

on account of race, color, or previous condition of servitude--

Section 2.
Congress shall have the power to enforce this article by appropriate legislation.

AMENDMENT XVI - Passed by Congress the second of July 1909. Ratified the third of February 1913.

> *Note: Article I, section 9, of the Constitution was modified by amendment 16.*

The Congress shall have the power to lay and collect taxes on incomes, from whatever source derived, without apportionment among the several States, and without any census or enumeration.

AMENDMENT XVII - Passed by Congress the thirteenth of May 1912. Ratified the eighth of April 1913.

> *Note: Article I, section 3, of the Constitution was modified by the 17th amendment.*

The Senate of the United States shall be composed of two Senators from each State, elected by the people thereof, and each Senator shall have one vote for six years. The electors in each State shall have the Qualifications requisite for electors of the most numerous branches of the State legislatures.

When vacancies happen in the representation of any State in the Senate, the executive authority of such State shall issue writs of election to fill such vacancies: Provided, That the Legislature of any State may empower the executive thereof to make temporary appointments until the people fill the vacancies by election as the Legislature may direct.

This amendment shall not be so construed as to affect the election or term of any Senator chosen before it becomes valid as part of the Constitution.

AMENDMENT XVIII - Passed by Congress on the eighteenth of December 1917. Ratified the sixteenth of January 1919. Repealed by amendment 21.

Section 1.
After one year from the ratification of this article, the manufacture, sale, or transportation of intoxicating liquors within, the importation thereof into, or the exportation thereof from the United States and all territory subject to the jurisdiction thereof for beverage purposes is hereby prohibited.

Section 2.
The Congress and the several States shall have concurrent power to enforce this article by appropriate legislation.

Section 3.
This article shall be inoperative unless it shall have been ratified as an amendment to the Constitution by the legislatures of the several States, as provided in the Constitution, within seven years from the date of the submission hereof to the States by the Congress.

AMENDMENT XIX - Passed by Congress the fourth of June 1919. Ratified the eighteenth of August 1920.

The right of citizens of the United States to vote shall not be denied or abridged by the United States or by any State on account of sex.

Congress shall have the power to enforce this article by appropriate legislation.

AMENDMENT XX - Passed by Congress the second of March 1932. Ratified the twenty-third of January 1933.

Note: Article I, section 4, of the Constitution was modified by section 2 of this amendment. In addition, a portion of the 12th amendment was superseded by section 3.

Section 1.
The terms of the President and the Vice President shall end at noon on the twentieth of January, and the terms of Senators and Representatives at noon on the third of January, of the years in which such terms would have ended if this article had not been ratified; and the terms of their successors shall then begin.

Section 2.
The Congress shall assemble at least once every year, and such meeting shall begin at noon on the third of January unless they shall by law appoint a different day.

Section 3.
If at the time fixed for the beginning of the term of the President, the President-elect shall have died, the Vice President-elect shall become President. If a President shall not have been chosen before the time fixed for the beginning of his term, or if the President-elect shall have

failed to qualify, then the Vice President-elect shall act as President until a President shall have qualified. The Congress may by law provide for the case wherein neither a President-elect nor a Vice President shall have qualified, declaring who shall then act as President, or the manner in which one who is to act shall be selected. Such person shall act accordingly until a President or Vice President shall have qualified.

Section 4.
The Congress may by law provide for the case of the death of any of the persons from whom the House of Representatives may choose a President whenever the right of choice shall have devolved upon them, and for the case of the death of any of the persons from whom the Senate may choose a Vice President whenever the right of choice shall have devolved upon them.

Section 5.
Sections 1 and 2 shall take effect on the fifteenth of October following the ratification of this article.

Section 6.
This article shall be inoperative unless it shall have been ratified as an amendment to the Constitution by the legislatures of three-fourths of the several States within seven years from its submission date.

AMENDMENT XXI - Passed by Congress the twentieth of February 1933. Ratified the fifth of December 1933.

Section 1.
The eighteenth article of amendment to the Constitution of the United States is hereby repealed.

Section 2.

The transportation or importation into any State, Territory, or Possession of the United States for delivery or use therein of intoxicating liquors, in violation of the laws thereof, is hereby prohibited.

Section 3.

This article shall be inoperative unless it shall have been ratified as an amendment to the Constitution by conventions in the several States, as provided in the Constitution, within seven years from the date of the submission hereof to the States by the Congress.

AMENDMENT XXII - Passed by Congress the twenty-first of March 1947. Ratified the twenty-seventh of February 1951.

Section 1.

No person shall be elected to the office of the President more than twice, and no person who has held the office of President, or acted as President, for more than two years of a term to which some other person was elected President shall be elected to the office of President more than once. But this article shall not apply to any person holding the office of President when this article was proposed by Congress, and shall not prevent any person who may be holding the office of President, or acting as President, during the term within which this article becomes operative from holding the office of President or acting as President during the remainder of such term.

Section 2.

This article shall be inoperative unless it shall have been ratified as an amendment to the Constitution by the legislatures of three-fourths of the several States within seven years from the date of its submission to the States by the Congress.

AMENDMENT XXIII - Passed by Congress on the sixteenth of June 1960. Ratified the twenty-ninth of March 1961.

Section 1.
The District constituting the seat of Government of the United States shall appoint in such manner as Congress may direct:

Several electors of President and Vice President equal to the whole number of Senators and Representatives in Congress to which the District would be entitled if it were a State, but in no event more than the least populous State; they shall be in addition to those appointed by the States, but they shall be considered, for the purposes of the election of President and Vice President, to be electors appointed by a State. They shall meet in the District and perform such duties as provided by the amendment's twelfth article.

Section 2.
Congress shall have the power to enforce this article by appropriate legislation.

AMENDMENT XXIV - Passed by Congress the twenty-seventh of August 1962. Ratified the twenty-third of January 1964.

Section 1.
The right of citizens of the United States to vote in any

primary or other election for President or Vice President, for electors for President or Vice President, or for Senator or Representative in Congress, shall not be denied or abridged by the United States or any State by reason of failure to pay a poll tax or other tax.

Section 2.
Congress shall have the power to enforce this article by appropriate legislation.

AMENDMENT XXV - Passed by Congress on the sixth of July 1965. Ratified the tenth of February 1967.

Note: Article II, section 1 of the Constitution, was affected by the 25th amendment.

Section 1.
In case of the removal of the President from office or of his death or resignation, the Vice President shall become President.

Section 2.
Whenever there is a vacancy in the vice president's office, the President shall nominate a Vice President who shall take office upon confirmation by a majority vote of both Houses of Congress.

Section 3.
Whenever the President transmits to the President pro tempore of the Senate and the Speaker of the House of Representatives his written declaration that he is unable to discharge the powers and duties of his office, and until he transmits to them a written declaration to the contrary, such

powers and duties shall be discharged by the Vice President as Acting President.

Section 4.
Whenever the Vice President and a majority of either the principal officers of the executive departments or of such other body as Congress may by law provide, transmit to the President pro tempore of the Senate and the Speaker of the House of Representatives their written declaration that the President is unable to discharge the powers and duties of his office, the Vice President shall immediately assume the powers and duties of the office as Acting President.

After that, when the President transmits to the President pro tempore of the Senate and the Speaker of the House of Representatives his written declaration that no inability exists, he shall resume the powers and duties of his office unless the Vice President and a majority of either the principal officers of the executive department or of such other body as Congress may by law provide, transmit within four days to the President pro tempore of the Senate and the Speaker of the House of Representatives their written declaration that the President is unable to discharge the powers and duties of his office. Thereupon Congress shall decide the issue, assembling within forty-eight hours for that purpose if not in session. If the Congress, within twenty-one days after receipt of the latter written declaration, or, if Congress is not in session, within twenty-one days after Congress is required to assemble, determines by two-thirds vote of both Houses that the President is unable to discharge the powers and duties of his office, the Vice President shall continue to discharge the same as Acting President; otherwise, the President shall resume the powers and duties of his office.

AMENDMENT XXVI - Passed by Congress the twenty-third of March 1971. Ratified the first of July 1971.

> *Note: Amendment 14, section 2, of the Constitution was modified by section 1 of the 26th amendment.*

Section 1.
The right of citizens of the United States, who are eighteen years of age or older, to vote shall not be denied or abridged by the United States or by any State on account of age.

Section 2.
Congress shall have the power to enforce this article by appropriate legislation.

AMENDMENT XXVII - Originally proposed the twenty-fifth of September 1789. Ratified the seventh of May 1992.

No law, varying the compensation for the Senators and Representatives' services, shall take effect until an election of representatives shall have intervened. [4]

---

[4] All Amendments to the United States Constitution. Accessed November 27, 2019. http://hrlibrary.umn.edu/education/all_amendments_usconst.htm.

The utmost thanks to all who have purchased "The Unfavorable Police Encounter" and for taking the time to educate yourselves on what to do if *you* ever find yourself in an unfavorable police encounter. Remember, not all police encounters are unfavorable. Police officers are positively serving their community every day in this country. As a police officer, I can attest that lives are being saved, the property is being recovered, and criminals are being arrested.

I hope this book has given you a better understanding of the criminal justice system. When you become involved, you'll have some knowledge of how to maneuver through the system and conduct yourself in the presence of police officers.

Also be aware Police Offices are making decisions along with Judges, State Attorneys, the Elective Officials, and Grand Jurors.

All of these sectors play a vital role in our criminal justice system.

Notes

Notes

Notes

Author's Bio

I was born and raised in Florida. I worked with Monticello Police Department; Tallahassee Police Department; Leon County Sheriff Department, as Deputy Sheriff; Dept of Corrections, as a Correction Officer; and Florida Highway Patrol for a total of 10 years. In conjunction with these careers, I served 30 years as a Military Police in the US Army and participated in Desert Storm and The War on Terror during his time of servicing our country. I also worked at the USPS for 27 years full-time. I am the father of three sons, and three grandchildren.

The information in this book gives an account of my experiences on the force and the community I served.

Contact Info

I'm available for speaking engagements at schools, organizations, and private events. For all comments, bulk purchases or any additional information and questions you may have, please contact me at:

Butlereugene725@gmail.com or

850-778-5328

Made in the USA
Columbia, SC
07 November 2021